Say I Am You

Say I Am You

 # RUMI

Poetry Interspersed with Stories of Rumi and Shams

translated by John Moyne and Coleman Barks

MAYPOP · Athens

Some of these poems appeared in *The Hand of Poetry*, Five Mystic Poets of Persia, with Lectures by Hazrat Inayat Khan, poetry translated by Coleman Barks, Omega Publications (New Lebanon, NY, 1993).

Maypop
196 Westview Drive
Athens, GA 30606
1-800-682-8637

Cover reproduced from 1989 Georgi calendar, "The Garden of Eichstaett," by permission of Verlag Dr. Rudolf Georgi, Aachen, Germany, and Georgi Publishers, Box 6059, Chelsea, MA 02150.

Designed & composed (in Monotype's PostScript rendition of old Fred Goudy's Truesdell typeface) by Moreland Hogan in Charlotte, North Carolina.

Printed & bound by Thomson-Shore, Inc., in Dexter, Michigan.

for Parvin and Nicholas

Contents

Sohbet

In sufi circles they say, "There's prayer, and a step up from that is meditation, and a step up from that is *sohbet*, or conversation." Who is talking to HU! (The pronoun for divine presence) Lover to beloved, teacher to disciple. The Friendship of Rumi and Shams became a continuous conversation, in silence and words, presence talking to absence, existence to non-existence, periphery to center. Rumi's poetry may be heard as eavesdropping on that exchange.

In 1244 Rumi was thirty-seven. We don't know how old Shams was when they met, maybe sixty, maybe forty-three. The ages do not matter. The intersection of these two searchers after truth, sometime in the fall of 1244, probably October, was a grand event in the mystical life of the planet. It opened a region, a companionship, that because of their intensity within it, can now be more completely experienced.

Who are these two? Jelaluddin Rumi was a scholar and an artist, the inheritor of a long learned line of theologians, and a venusian appreciator of God's beauty. Shams was a sudden, elusive warrior who demanded everything this life could give. He prayed for a companion to his soul. "What will you give in return?" a voice asked. "My head!" "The one you seek is Jelaluddin of Konya." So a bargain was struck in the invisible world. Fire met fire, ocean ocean, in a small square in south-central Anatolia. There is no explaining the place of pure being they went to together. Perhaps a fragrance comes in the poetry.

Theirs is the story of longing for company on the Way. The

searching, the meeting, the enjoyment of mysterious conversation, the wrenching away, and the transmutation of absence to another level of presence. Language, music, and movement spring from the various stages of separation and union. There is continuous re-formation until what is looked for is the jewel-light in the eye of the looker. Rumi and Shams were together for three and a half years. Twice Shams was forced into exile, and he was finally murdered by a clique of jealous disciples. Poetry broke from Rumi's grief, a plangent night-calling, that turned into knowledge that their Friendship could become his very being. "This poetry is elusive because that presence is." The joyful expansiveness, expert fumbling, and perfect wandering of Rumi's art brings new freedom and intimacy to poetry and to the community where it can be lived. Simple playfulness and the most severe truth walk along here in harmony. The paradox of this poetry is that it takes place in the most private region, an area of experience that cannot be shared, and yet that is what it attempts, even as it preserves the secrecy of the conversation. Rinzai Zen employs a method of "instant dialogue" between teacher and student, which leads through astonishment and irrationality to a new understanding of reality. The *sohbet* of Rumi and Shams has some of this deft spontaneity as well as the longing we associate with the sufi way.

The stories of Rumi and Shams included here are true in the same place the poems are true, the world where soul and spirit growth merges with form. I enjoy especially the incidents involving animals. Rumi felt deep rapport with dogs and ducks and heifers, and how they resonate with people. He spoke directly to that, which is why we listen to him as we do, with wonder and with a willingness to obey the gentle imperatives.

Sohbet is receptivity, but not only that. It is the daring to carry on lively, spontaneous dialogue with the teacher. A profound listening, and also the dignity of reply. *Sohbet* is the silence where Rumi and Shams live the humor and the joy and the freedom, a Friendship called *Mevlana*.

Coleman Barks
May 2, 1994

A Note on these Translations

John Moyne, Persian scholar and Emeritus Professor of
Linguistics at the City University of New York, and Coleman
Barks, poet and Associate Professor of English at the University
of Georgia, collaborate to produce many of these free verse
translations. The rest come from Coleman Barks' work with the
scholarly translations of Reynold Nicholson and A. J. Arberry.
The Sultan Velad poem was done with Alan Godlas of the
Religion Department of the University of Georgia.

Love Dogs

One night a man was crying,
                    Allah! Allah!
His lips grew sweet with the praising,
until a cynic said,
                    "So! I have heard you
calling out, but have you ever
gotten any response?"

The man had no answer to that.
He quit praying and fell into a confused sleep.

He dreamed he saw Khidr, the guide of souls,
in a thick, green foliage.
                    "Why did you stop praising?"
"Because I've never heard anything back."
                    "This longing

you express *is* the return message."

The grief you cry out from
draws you toward union.

Your pure sadness
that wants help
is the secret cup.

Listen to the moan of a dog for its master.
That whining is the connection.

There are love-dogs
no one knows the names of.

Give your life
to be one of them.

Majnun with Layla's Dog

Majnun saw Layla's dog and began kissing it,
running around like a hajji circling the Kaaba,
bowing to its paws, holding its head, scratching
its stomach, giving it sweets and rosewater.

"You idiot," said someone passing by.
"Dogs lick their privates and sniff
excrement on the road. This is *insane*,
the intimate way you treat that dog."

"Look through my eyes," said the lover.
"See the loyalty, how he guards the house
of my Friend, how he's so glad to see us.

Whatever we feel, grief, the simple delight
of being out in the sun, he feels
that with us completely.

Don't look too much at surface actions.
Discover the lion, the rose of his real nature.
Friend, this dog is a garden gate into the invisible."

Anyone preoccupied with pointing out what's wrong
misses the unseen. Look at his face!

Looking for the ocean, I find
a shell with a piece of foam on it.

I taste the ocean in the foam,
turn, and the steep trail
opens on a high plain.

> Your eyes are the mystery, with thousands
> of lives living in the edges.
>
> Your hair full of forgetfulness,
> your face pure praise.
>
> So clarity is decorated
> with mistakes!

Not until someone dissolves,
can he or she know
what union is.

That descends only
into emptiness.

A lie does not change to truth
with just talking about it.

Soul of this world,
no life, nor world remain,
no beautiful women and men longing,
only this ancient love

circling the holy black stone of nothing,
where the lover is the love,
the horizon, and everything within it.

You who long for powerful positions,
keep worrying about that, and your land!

We burn inside union
with one truth,

There is no reality but God.
There's only God.

A poet tries to say love's mystery,
why the reed flute grieves.

Listen and obey
the hushed language.
Go naked.

There's no light like yours. No breeze
quick enough to carry your fragrance.

When intelligence leaves its castle
and walks through your lane,

it doesn't know where or who it is.
It sits on the ground and babbles.

As salt dissolves in ocean,
I was swallowed up in you,
beyond doubt or being sure.

Suddenly here in my chest a star
came out so clear, it drew
all stars into it.

Love told me to reject mind,
and also spirit. *Live with me.*

For a while, I did. Then I left,
came back, and left again.
Now I'm here to stay.

Spring

Again, the violet bows to the lily.
Again, the rose is tearing off her gown!

The green ones have come from the other world,
tipsy like the breeze up to some new foolishness.

Again, near the top of the mountain
the anemone's sweet features appear.

The hyacinth speaks formally to the jasmine,
"Peace be with you." "And peace to you, lad!
Come walk with me in this meadow."

Again, there are sufis everywhere!

The bud is shy, but the wind removes
her veil suddenly, "My friend!"

The Friend is here like water in the stream,
like a lotus on the water.

The narcissus winks at the wysteria,
"Whenever you say."

And the clove to the willow, "You are the one
I hope for." The willow replies, "Consider
these chambers of mine yours. Welcome!"

The apple, "Orange, why the frown?"
"So that those who mean harm
will not see my beauty."

The ringdove comes asking, "Where,
where is the Friend?"

With one note the nightingale
indicates the rose.

Again, the *season* of Spring has come
and a spring-source rises under everything,
a moon sliding from the shadows.

Many things must be left unsaid, because it's late,
but whatever conversation we haven't had
tonight, we'll have tomorrow.

The Source of Joy

No one knows what makes the soul
wake up so happy!

Maybe a dawn breeze has blown the veil
from the face of God.

A thousand new moons appear.
Roses open laughing,

Hearts become perfect rubies
like those from Badakshan.

The body turns entirely spirit.
Leaves become branches in this wind!

Why is it now so easy to surrender,
even for those already surrendered?

There's no answer to any of this.
No one knows the source of joy.

A poet breathes into a reed flute,
and the tip of every hair makes music.

Shams sails down clods of dirt from the roof,
and we take jobs as doorkeepers for him.

The One Thing You Must Do

There is one thing in this world which you must never forget to
do. If you forget everything else and not this, there's nothing to
worry about, but if you remember everything else and forget this,
then you will have done nothing in your life.

It's as if a king has sent you to some country to do a task, and you
perform a hundred other services, but not the one he sent you
to do. So human beings come to this world to do *particular work*.
That work is the purpose, and each is specific to the person. If you
don't do it, it's as though a priceless Indian sword were used to
slice rotten meat. It's a golden bowl being used to cook turnips,
when one filing from the bowl could buy a hundred suitable pots.
It's like a knife of the finest tempering nailed into a wall to hang
things on.

You say, "But look, I'm using the dagger. It's not lying idle."
Do you hear how ludicrous that sounds? For a penny an iron
nail could be bought to serve for that. You say, "But I spend my
energies on lofty enterprises. I study jurisprudence and philosophy
and logic and astronomy and medicine and all the rest." But
consider why you do those things. They are all branches of
yourself.

Remember the deep root of your being, the presence of your lord.
Give your life to the one who already owns your breath and your
moments. If you don't, you will be exactly like the man who takes
a precious dagger and hammers it into his kitchen wall for a peg
to hold his dipper gourd. You'll be wasting valuable keenness and
foolishly ignoring your dignity and your purpose.

Stories of Shams and Rumi

Shams wandered the world looking for a companion, a Friend on his level of attainment. Sometimes, for three or four days he would be lost in mystical awareness. Then he would take work as a mason, or a mason's helper, to balance his visionary bewilderment with hard physical labor. When he was paid, he would always contrive to slip the wages into another worker's jacket before he left. He never stayed anywhere long. Whenever students began to assemble around him, as they inevitably did, he would excuse himself for a drink of water, wrap his black cloak around, and be gone.

Some say that Rumi and Shams met in Damascus before their meeting in Konya. They jostled against each other in the market. Their eyes met. "Who are you?" asked Rumi. "I am the money-changer of the world!" replied Shams. Rumi turned his head away for a moment, puzzled. When he looked back Shams had dissolved into the crowd. Soon after this mysterious glance, Rumi, under the guidance of Burhan Mahaqqiq, did three consecutive *chillas* (a forty-day fast with only a pot of water and two or three loaves of barleybread.) He showed no signs of suffering during this time, and Burhan pronounced him perfect in all science, human and spiritual.

Shams arrived in Konya sometime in the fall of 1244. He took lodging at an inn, pretending to be a successful merchant, a seller of sugar, though in his room there was only a broken water pot, a ragged mat, and a headrest of unbaked clay. He fasted continually, breaking it once every ten or twelve days with bread soaked in mutton broth.

Shams was a disciple of a certain basket maker in Tabriz, Ruknaddin Sanjabi, but he traveled all over the region to find and hear the deepest teachers. Because of this restless searching, his nickname was *Parinda*, or "the flier," or "bird." He prayed that God's hidden favorite be revealed to him, so that he could learn more of the mysteries of divine love. Jelaluddin, the son of Bahauddin of Balkh, was revealed to be the one he sought, and Konya the place where he lived. One day as Shams sat at the gate of the inn, Rumi came riding by on a donkey, surrounded by a crowd of students. Shams rose and took hold of the bridle, "Money-changer of the current coins of esoteric significance, knower of the names of the lord, tell me! Who was greater, Muhammed or Bestami?" "Muhammed was incomparable among the prophets and saints." "Then how is it he said, 'We have not known You as You should be known,' while Bestami cried out, 'How great is my glory!'" Rumi fainted when he heard the depth the question came from, and fell to the ground. When he revived, he answered, "For Muhammed the mystery was always unfolding, while Bestami took one gulp and was satisfied." The two tottered off together and were closeted for weeks and months at a time in that mystical conversation called *sohbet*.

The sudden absorption of their teacher with the wild dervish troubled Rumi's disciples, and eventually they became so jealous that Shams was forced to leave. Rumi sent his son, Sultan Velad, to bring him back. There was further plotting against Shams, and some time in 1246 he disappeared altogether. Rumi adopted as mourning clothes the drab tombstone hat and wide black cloak still worn by the Mevlevi today.

Once Shams was located in Damascus, in a tavern gambling at cards with a young westerner, who is traditionally identified as Francis of Assisi. Young Francis was cheating Shams. But when Rumi's son and his entourage entered paying homage to Shams as a great emperor of the spirit, Francis immediately confessed and gave Shams back the money. "No. You must keep it and give it to the Friends in the West." So a beautiful bond was made, acknowledging the truth at the core where all religions connect.

Kira Khatun, Rumi's wife and "the Mary of her age," peered through a slit in the door, into the room where Shams and Rumi were sitting in spiritual communion. She saw one of the walls open and six majestic beings enter. The strangers bowed and laid flowers at Rumi's feet, although it was the middle of winter. They remained until the time for dawn prayers, which they motioned for Shams to lead. He excused himself, and Rumi performed the duties. When the prayers were over, the six left through the wall. Rumi came from the chamber and seeing his wife in the hall, gave her the flowers. "Some visitors brought these for you."

The next day she sent her servant to the perfumer's market with a few leaves and blossoms from the bouquet. The perfumers were baffled, unable to identify the flowers, until a spice trader from India recognized them as varieties that grew only in Ceylon. The servant went back with this astonishing news, and just as he was telling it, Rumi came in and told her to take good care of the flowers, because Indian saints had brought them from the paradise that human beings had lost. As long as Kira Khatun lived, the flowers stayed fresh and fragrant, and just a single leaf applied to a diseased eye, or other injured part, brought instantaneous healing.

There was a young man in Konya, a merchant. His house was close to Rumi's college, and he himself felt profoundly connected with Mevlana. But a strong desire came on him to travel to Egypt. His friends tried to dissuade him, and when Rumi heard of the plan, he also gently opposed the idea. The young man, though, was too restless to follow any advice. He secretly left Konya in the middle of the night and went to Antioch on the coast of Syria. There he embarked on a ship going to Egypt. The ship was boarded on the high seas by pirates, and the young man was taken to their stronghold, put in an underground dungeon, and fed just enough to stay alive. Forty days he was held in these conditions. On the night of the fortieth day, Rumi visited him in a dream and said, "Tomorrow, no matter what they ask you, reply, 'I know.' If you do this, you'll be released."

He woke bewildered and grateful. He sat meditating in his cell, waiting for the solution to be given. Very soon a crowd came with an interpreter and asked, "Do you know anything of the healing arts? Our leader is sick." The young man answered, "I know." Immediately they led him out and bathed and dressed him handsomely and took him to the residence of the ailing man. There, Rumi revealed the cure to the young man through his own intuitions. He asked for seven fruits. He crushed them together and added scammony to the juices and the pulp. He gave this concoction to the patient for three days. The pirate chieftain recovered, summoned the young man, and told him to ask for whatever he wanted. He asked for his freedom and the means to return to Konya, where his master lived. Then he told the story of what had happened: his desire to go to Egypt, his disobeying Rumi's advice, the dream-vision, the cure. Those that heard became such lovers of Rumi that they gave the young man gifts to take back to Konya. When he arrived, he saw Rumi's face from far off. He ran and kissed his feet and wept. Rumi raised the young man up and kissed him, "That was a narrow escape with the pirates! Saying you could cure their leader was risky! Your absconding from here brought you the chaos of the open sea, the vicious attack, and the dark confinement underground. Stay here with us for a while now where you feel more peaceful and content. Let contentment guide you. Study and accept the blessings being given."

Which Way Does the Night Go?

Love comes with a knife, not some shy question,
and not with fears for its reputation!

I say these things disinterestedly.
Accept them in kind.

Love is a madman,
working his wild schemes,
tearing off his clothes, running
through the mountains, drinking poison,
and now quietly choosing annihilation.

A tiny spider tries to wrap an enormous wasp.
Think of the spiderweb woven across
the cave where Muhammed slept!

There are love stories,
and there is obliteration into love.

You've been walking the ocean's edge,
holding up your robes to keep them dry.

You must dive naked under, and deeper
under, a thousand times deeper!

Love flows down. The ground submits
to the sky and suffers what comes.

Tell me, is the earth worse
for giving in like that?

Don't put blankets over the drum!
Open completely. Let your spirit-ear
listen to the green dome's passionate murmur.

Let the cords of your robe be untied. Shiver
in this new love beyond all above and below.

The sun rises, but which way does the night go?
I have no more words.

Let the soul speak
with the silent articulation
of a face.

Any Chance Meeting

In every gathering, in any chance meeting
on the street, there is a shine,
an elegance rising-up.

Today, I recognized that that jewel-like beauty
is the presence, our loving confusion,
the glow in which watery clay
gets brighter than fire,

the one we call the Friend.
I begged, "Is there a way into you,
a ladder?"
            "Your head is the ladder.
Bring it down under your feet."
                            The mind, this globe
of awareness, is a starry universe that when
you push off from it with your foot,

a thousand new roads come clear, as you yourself
do at dawn, sailing through the light.

Where Are All the Others?

Those full of fear are not really on the way.
Everyone here is a king. No servants.

The wave can never be afraid of the ocean.
Inside that motion, how can anything be "other?"

When you feel separate, you're in your imagination.
Saints are the lights we see within this

exquisite fluid, and I'm not talking
about the elements! There's a light

that's the opposite of fire, as white to black.
When what I'm pointing to arrives,

there's no trace of burning. Don't ask
for a lineage of revelation, or explication

of texts, or rules of morality. There's nothing
here but love and mystery. Welcome to the tavern

where drunkards get sober and transparent,
until they disappear altogether in the face

of the one they love. Whatever loosens the taste
of their joy comes new with each breath.

In this orchard, and for the garden we farm,
there's no summer or winter. Roses open

every direction. This world's existence
is one night long. There's a great lively

gathering that night, but some people sleep
through it. Anyone who has seen the Beloved

wonders, "Where are all the others?" This
has nothing to do with thinking or belief.

Bahauddin, you've been left here alone
without your father, the great Mevlana.

From now on you'll have no friend,
no form to love, only what's real.

Flag-Lions

You see flag-lions playing in the wind,
leaping about, but you don't see wind.

You can say if it's an east wind or a west,
healthy or destructive, but little else.

The body is like the lion on the banner.
Vital weather blows and makes it dance,

and then die down. The flag-lion
drops its haunches and looks up.

There is an invisible reality
the closed eye sees in dream,

a sun and a moon. Spirit, a perfection,
shines inside our nights and days.

Sleep is death's brother, but there are
many varieties of sleep. Learn about them!

Some people behold, sleeping, representations
of an awareness they will not reach, awake,

for twenty years. They run to scholarly
dream-interpreters, more out of curiosity

than anything else. Stay in the root
of your dream. Don't climb out on

intellectual branches. We need robust elephants
who lay down lost in a vision of Hindustan.

Remember and return are not pulling everyone,
just those deep-desiring elephants.

Donkeys never dream of India. But you can become
an elephant, even if you're a donkey now!

Unseen alchemists speak of this in your ear
every moment. Listen to them. Feel

their touchings. Discover the new healing
plants that come up at dawn. Study

the life of Ibrahim, who changed suddenly
because of what he saw in his sleep.

He cut the ropes that held him and began wandering,
as Muhammed said, somewhere between the sad

attachments of the senses and a pure
union with light. Your own transformation,

like the play of wind with a flag, moves
in you now, that near, that simple.

Personal Intelligence

Your personal intelligence is not capable of doing
work. It can learn, but it cannot create.

That must come from non-time, non-space.
Real work begins there.

Mind does its fine-tuning hair-splitting,
but no craft or art begins
or can continue without a Master
giving wisdom into it.

A Zero-Circle

Be helpless and dumbfounded,
unable to say yes or no.

Then a stretcher will come
from grace to gather us up.

We are too dulleyed to see the beauty.
If we say *Yes we can,* we'll be lying.

If we say *No, we don't see it,*
that *No* will behead us
and shut tight our window into spirit.

So let us not be sure of anything,
beside ourselves, and only that, so
miraculous beings come running to help.

Crazed, lying in a zero-circle, mute,
we will be saying finally,
with tremendous eloquence, *Lead us.*

When we've totally surrendered to that beauty,
we'll become a mighty kindness.

The Sign of Being Dried-Up

The sign of being a dried-up branch,
unconnected to root-water in the deep ground,
is that you have no inclination to sway.

Moist, fresh limbs are easily pulled
any direction, even rounded into
a hoop for a basket handle.

This is symbolic talk, but the symbol itself
is a fire to consume your fantasies
about how you are in union.

Be empty as you go into
qualities and essence.

Some letters disappear when they elide.
That way the true meaning emerges.

No words can express how inspired
words spring out of silence.

Be Suspicious of Yourself

Everything you do has a quality
which comes back to you in some way.

Every action takes a form in the invisible world,
which may be different from how you thought

it would appear. A crime is committed,
and a gallows begins to be built. One does not

look like the other, but they correspond.
Accept the results of what you've done in anger,

or for greed, or to elevate your ego. Don't blame
fate! That dog lies in the kennel

and will not respond to anyone's calling.
Be suspicious of yourself! Inquire

about your hidden motives. It takes courage
to repent, and more courage to change.

But realize this: just as dustgrains shine
in sunlight coming through this window,

so there's a light of reality, within which ideas,
hidden hypocrisies, and the qualities

of every action become clear. All you've done
and will do will be seen in the light of that sun.

The Waterwheel

In this river the soul is a waterwheel
that no matter how it's facing, water pours
through, turning, re-turning to the river.

Even if you put your side
or your back to the river,
water still comes through.

A shadow can't ignore the sun
that all day creates and moves it!

The soul lives like a drop of mercury
in the palm of a palsied man.

Or say the soul is the moon,
that every thirty nights has two
so empty, in union, that it disappears.

The other twenty-eight nights it endures
different stages of separation,
wretched, but laughing.

Laughter is the way of lovers.
They live and die tickled,

and always fresh-faced, knowing
the return that's coming.

Don't question this! The answers
and your questions in response

will cause your eyes to see wrongly.
Live the laughing silence.

A Trace

You that give new life to this planet,
you that transcend logic, come.

I am only an arrow. Fill your bow
with me and let fly!

Because of this love for you,
my bowl has fallen from the roof.

Put down a ladder,
and collect the pieces, please!

People ask, "But which roof is your roof?"
I answer, "Wherever the soul came from
and wherever it goes at night,

my roof is in that direction! From wherever
Spring arrives to heal the ground, from
wherever searching rises in a human being."

The looking itself is a *trace*
of what we're looking for,

but we've been more like the man who sat on his donkey
and asked the donkey where to go!

Be quiet now and wait.
It may be that the ocean one, that we desire so
to move into and become,

desires us out here on land a little longer,
going our sundry roads to the shore.

What Hurts the Soul?

We tremble, thinking we're about to dissolve
into non-existence, but non-existence fears
even more that it might be given human form!

Loving God is the only pleasure.
Other delights turn bitter.

What hurts the soul?
To live without tasting
the water of its own essence.

People focus on death and this material earth.
They have doubts about soul-water.
Those doubts can be reduced!

Use night to wake your clarity.
Darkness and the living water are lovers.
Let them stay up together.

When merchants eat their big meals and sleep
their dead sleep, we night-thieves go to work.

The Guest-House

This being human is a guest-house.
Every morning a new arrival.

A joy, a depression, a meanness,
some momentary awareness comes
as an unexpected visitor.

Welcome and entertain them all!
Even if they're a crowd of sorrows,
who violently sweep your house
empty of its furniture,

still, treat each guest honorably.
He may be clearing you out
for some new delight.

The dark thought, the shame, the malice,
meet them at the door laughing,
and invite them in.

Be grateful for whoever comes,
because each has been sent
as a guide from beyond.

Is This a Stage Set?

Ask someone whose house this is,
where music continues to flow out.

Is this the Kaaba, or a temple of light?
Is there something here
that the universe cannot hold?

Or is this a stage set?
Don't tear it down!

And don't try to talk to the owner.
He's asleep.

Make perfume of the dust and the trash
here, where the framing is poetry,
the kitchen talk pure praise!

Whoever enters this room becomes wise.
This is the house of love,
where no one can distinguish leaf
from blossom or trap from bait.
Everything mirrors everything here.

The hairtip sinks through the comb.
No one knows anyone's name.

Don't wait on the doorsill!
Walk this forest full of lions,
and don't consider the danger.

No need to set fires everywhere you go.
The lion's thicket is silence.
Speech, a flame.

Solomon's Crooked Crown

Solomon was busy judging others,
when it was his personal thoughts
that were disrupting the community.

His crown slid crooked on his head.
He put it straight, but the crown went
awry again. Eight times this happened.

Finally he began to talk to his headpiece.
"Why do you keep tilting over my eyes?"

"I have to. When your power loses compassion,
I have to show what such a condition looks like."

Immediately Solomon recognized the truth.
He knelt and asked forgiveness.
The crown centered itself on his crown.

When something goes wrong, accuse yourself first.
Even the wisdom of Plato or Solomon
can wobble and go blind.

Listen when your crown reminds you
of what makes you cold toward others,
as you pamper the greedy energy inside.

Stories of Rumi and Shams

There was a woman in Konya named Fehrunnisa, which means "the glory of women." She often participated in the meetings at Rumi's house, and he often visited hers. They were great companions in their love for God. Some of Fehrunnisa's friends suggested that she go on hajj. She said she would consult with Jelaluddin about it. As she entered his presence, he called out, "Great idea! Have a fine journey. God willing, we'll go together!" She heard, but said nothing. The others present were baffled by this exchange. That night she stayed as a guest, deep in conversation with Rumi until midnight, when he went up on the roof to worship and perform the vigil. As he finished praying, he fell into an ecstatic trance, sighing and shouting. He lifted the skylight to the room below and called Fehrunnisa to join him. As she came up onto the roof, she saw very plainly the cube of the Kaaba turning in the sky like a dervish, every detail perfectly clear. She screamed out in joy and lost consciousness. When she revived, she realized she did not need to make the trip to Mecca.

Rumi was walking by the moat around the edge of Konya when a group of students from a neighboring college posed a question they thought would confuse him, "What color was the dog who slept in the cave with the seven sleepers?" Rumi's spontaneous answer was, "Light yellow. A lover is always pale with longing, as I am, and that dog was a lover." They followed along then asking questions that were less impudent.

Two men quarreling in the street: "Go ahead! Say whatever you want! I have a thousand words to answer every one that you say!" Rumi stepped between them, "No, say them to me. For every thousand you give, you'll hear back just one." The two men made peace.

A certain rich man and his wife were disciples of Rumi. The man went on hajj, and while he was gone, the wife made a delicious meal and sent it in a distinctive china bowl to Jelaluddin, asking that as he ate of it to please remember her husband with a blessing. Rumi and his disciples feasted on the food. They ate all of it, and yet the bowl remained full. Rumi said, "Oh, he must have some too." He took the dish to the terraced roof and came back empty-handed. When asked what he'd done with the food, he replied, "I gave the bowl to her husband, since it belongs to him." No one knew what he meant, but in due time the pilgrims returned and the same piece of china was found in the merchant's baggage. "How did you get this?" the wife asked. "Ah! I was eating dinner with the others, when an arm projected through the tent-flap, placed this bowl full of beautiful food before me, then withdrew. I sent servants to learn who had done this, but no one could be found." The two went to Rumi weeping for joy at the generosity shown them. "The whole series of events rose from your love and your trust," replied Rumi. "God has merely used my hand as an instrument to make them more manifest."

Shams and Rumi loved to sit together and play chess. One day when Rumi saw that he was about to be put in a position where eventually there was no way to avoid checkmate, he called out in mock despair, "I am lost!" Shams replied from the inner realm they shared, "No, you have won." Rumi immediately received a deeper realization from his teacher.

Rumi gave his disciples several reasons for the use of poetry and music in his community. "Responding to the prayers of the first Caliph, Abu Bakr, God made the Romans a major recipient of his mercy and Roman Anatolia (western and central Turkey) the most beautiful of all landscapes. The people here, though, could not receive such grace. They had little taste for the inner life or the unseen world. For that reason, I was attracted away from Khorasan (Persia), so that my children in this community could change the Roman copper to gold. They themselves would become the philosopher stones which cause this alchemy. But since Roman Anatolia was not ready for the gifts I had to give, I devised poetry, with music, to entrance the inhabitants toward spiritual truth. The people who live in this region are very blessed, lively and curious and fond of art, but as a sick child must be coaxed with sweetening to take medicine, they must be persuaded with poetry to acquire a longing for the soul."

There was a night-meeting of eminent citizens at the palace. As was the custom, each brought a large cylinder of candlewax, weighing four or five pounds, to burn during the discussion. Rumi brought a small taper. The meeting began with everyone smiling sweetly at Mevlana's small candle. "Your imposing lights, though," he commented quietly, "depend on mine." They smiled even wider. Rumi blew his out, and the company was sitting in darkness. After a short while in the silence they heard him sigh. His candle caught from the breath, and all the candles ignited as before. Many of those present became disciples that evening.

One of his dervishes died, and the family came to Rumi to ask if he should be buried in a coffin or without one. Rumi told them to do as they felt best, but Kerimuddin, another disciple, commented, "To be buried without a coffin is preferable, because a mother can nurse her child better than the child's brother. The ground is our mother. The wood of a coffin grows from the ground and so is the earth's child as we are. A corpse should be given to the loving parent directly." Rumi expressed admiration for this sublime doctrine, which, he said, was not to be found in any book.

One day Rumi asked one of his young disciples to bring him a great dish of rich and delicious food. The young man was alarmed because he thought that Rumi was living as an ascetic. Rumi used to pray all night and eat hardly anything. "What he really wants is to go off secretly and eat all this food!" The disciple secretly followed Rumi as he carried the food through the streets of Konya and out into the fields and into the ruins of a tomb. "Now I'll unmask his pretentions!" But what the young disciple found was an exhausted mother dog with six puppies. Rumi was feeding her by hand so that she could care for her children. "But how did you know that she was here, and hungry?" Rumi laughed, "When you have become awake, your ears are so sensitive they can hear the cries of a sparrow ten thousand miles away."

The Reed Flute's Song

Listen to the story told by the reed,
of being separated.

"Since I was cut from the reedbed,
I have made this crying sound.

Anyone apart from someone he loves
understands what I say.

Anyone pulled from a source
longs to go back.

At any gathering I am there,
mingling in the laughing and grieving,

a friend to each, but few
will hear the secrets hidden

within the notes. No ears for that.
body flowing out of spirit,

spirit up from body: no concealing
that mixing. But it's not given us

to see the soul. The reed flute
is fire, not wind. Be that empty."

Hear the love-fire tangled
in the reed notes, as bewilderment

melts into wine. The reed is a friend
to all who want the fabric torn

and drawn away. The reed is hurt
and salve combining. Intimacy

and longing for intimacy, one
song. A disasterous surrender,

and a fine love, together.
The one who secretly hears this

is senseless. A tongue has
one customer, the ear.

If a sugarcane flute had no effect,
it would not have been able to make sugar

in the reedbed. Whatever sound
it makes is for everyone.

Days full of wanting, let them go by
without worrying that they do.

Stay where you are, inside
such a pure, hollow note.

Every thirst gets satisfied except
that of these fish, the mystics,

who swim an ocean of grace
still somehow longing for it!

No one lives in that without
being nourished every day.

But if someone doesn't want
to hear the song of the reed flute,

it's best to cut conversation
short, say goodbye, and leave.

The Animal Soul

There's part of us that's like an itch.
Call it the *animal soul*, a foolishness
that when we're in it, we make
hundreds of others around us itchy.

And there is an intelligent soul
with another desire, more like sweet basil,
or the feel of a breeze.

Listen and be thankful even for scolding
that comes from the intelligent soul.
It flows out close to where you flowed out.

But that itchiness wants to put food
in our mouths that will make us sick,

feverish with the aftertaste of kissing
a donkey's rump. It's like blackening your robe
against a kettle without being anywhere
near a table of companionship.

The truth of a being human is an empty table
made of soul-intelligence.

Gradually reduce what you give your animal soul,
the bread that after all overflows from sunlight.

The animal soul itself spilled out
and sprouted from the other.

Taste more often what nourishes your clear light,
and you'll have less use for the smoky oven.

You'll bury that baking equipment in the ground!

The Womb

There is no prison so dark and small
as your mother's womb was,
and yet a window opened there,
from which you saw into the presence.

You felt infinite delight.
You wanted to stay.

This is the secret of spiritual pleasure:
the way goes in. These buildings
are just false fronts.

One man curls up in rapture
in an outside nook of a mosque.

Another walks disappointedly
his elegant gardens.

A Song of Being Empty

A certain sufi tore his robe in grief,
and the tearing brought such relief,

he gave the robe the name *faraji*,
which means *ripped open*, or *happiness*,
or *one who brings the joy of being opened*.

It comes from the stem *faraj*, which also
refers to *the genitals, male and female*.

His teacher understood the purity
of the action, while others
just saw the ragged appearance.

If you want peace and purity,
tear away your coverings.

This is the purpose of emotion, to let
a streaming beauty flow through you.

Call it spirit, elixir, or the original
agreement between yourself and God.

Opening into that gives peace,
a song of being empty,
pure silence.

Needle and Thread

What is a living death?

When you forget the spiritual life of the one
who teaches you, and that life is nothing but
wisdom come upon in suffering and difficulties.

The more of that knowing
you have the more soul.

How are we above animals?

Just with that same consciousness
that builds in us in times of trial.

There is a hierarchy: human over animal, angel over
human, and true human beings, the sheikhs,
the teachers, are above angels.

Why else would the angels be commanded
to bow before Adam?

Does a rose bow to a thorn?
Let your soul follow a one-pointed,
perfected human as thread follows needle.

The Water You Want

Someone may be clairvoyant, able to see
the future, and yet have very little wisdom.

Like the man who saw water in his dream,
and began leading everyone toward the mirage.

"I am the one with heart-vision.
I've torn open the veil."

So they set out with him inside the dream,
while he is actually sleeping beside a river
of pure water. Any search moves away from
the spot where the object of the quest is.

Sleep deeply wherever you are on the way.
Maybe some traveler will wake you.

Give up subtle thinking, the twofold, threefold
multiplication of mistakes. Listen to
the sound of waves within you.

There you are, dreaming your thirst,
when the water you want is
inside the big vein
on your neck.

The Reasonable Father

The universe is a form of divine law,
your reasonable father.

When you feel ungrateful to him,
the shapes of the world seem mean and ugly.

Make peace with that father, the elegant patterning,
and every experience will fill with immediacy.

Because I love this, I am never bored.
Beauty constantly wells up, a noise of springwater
in my ear and in my inner being.

Tree limbs rise and fall like the ecstatic arms
of those who have submitted to the mystical life.

Leaf-sounds talk together like poets
making fresh metaphors. The green felt cover slips,
and we get a flash of the mirror underneath.

Think how it will be when the whole thing
is pulled away! I tell only one one-thousandth
of what I see, because there's so much doubt everywhere.

The conventional opinion of this poetry is,
it shows great optimism for the future.

But Father Reason says,
No need to announce the future!
This now is it. *This.* Your deepest need and desire
is satisfied by the *moment's* energy
here in your hand.

Hypothesis and Human Being

Before Muhammed appeared in physical form,
there were many who loved the texts
that described his coming.

Imagination flourished. "We wait for that one,"
they prayed to this hypothetical being.

Then he took an actual shape,
and most of them left like the wind.

Muhammed is a true mirror. No one enjoys
being shown his or her hypocrisy.

Try not to stand for long before some surface
that keeps your faults hidden.

Polishing the Mirror

When Abu Bakr met Muhammed, he said,
"This is not a face that lies."

Abu Bakr was one whose bowl
has fallen from the roof.

There's no hiding the fragrance that comes
from an ecstatic. A polished mirror
cannot help reflecting.

Muhammed once was talking to a crowd
of chieftains, princes with great influence,
when a poor blind man interrupted him.

Muhammed frowned and said to the man,
"Let me attend to these visitors.
This is a rare chance,
whereas you are already my friend.
We'll have ample time."

Then someone nearby said, "That blind man
may be worth a hundred kings. Remember
the proverb, *Human beings are mines.*"

World-power means nothing. Only the unsayable,
jeweled inner life matters.

Muhammed replied, "Do not think that I'm concerned
with being acknowledged by these authorities.

If a beetle moves toward rosewater, it proves
that the solution is diluted. Beetles
love dung, not rose-essence.

If a coin is eager to be tested
by the touchstone, that coin
itself may be a touchstone.

A thief loves the night.
I am day. I reveal essences.

A calf thinks God is a cow.
A donkey's theology changes
when someone new pets it
and gives what it wants.

I am not a cow, or thistles for camels
to browse on. People who insult me
are only polishing the mirror."

A Star Without a Name

When a baby is taken from the wet nurse,
it easily forgets her
and starts eating solid food.

Seeds feed awhile on ground,
then lift up into the sun.

So you should taste the filtered light
and work your way toward wisdom
with no personal covering.

That's how you came here, like a star
without a name. Move across the nightsky
with those anonymous lights.

Talking Through the Door

You said, "Who's at the door?"
      I said, "Your slave."

You said, "What do you want?"
      "To see you and bow."

"How long will you wait?"
      "Until you call."

"How long will you cook?"
      "Till the resurrection."

We talked through the door. I claimed
a great love and that I had given up
what the world gives to be in that love.

You said, "Such claims require a witness."
      I said, "This longing, these tears."

You said, "Discredited witnesses."
      I said, "Surely not!"

You said, "Who did you come with?"
      "This majestic imagination you gave me."

"Why did you come?"
      "The musk or your wine was in the air."

"What is your intention?"
      "Friendship."

"What do you want from me?"
      "Grace."

Then you asked, "Where have you been most comfortable?"
      "In the palace."

"What did you see there?"
       "Amazing things."

"Then why is it so desolate?"
       "Because all that can be taken away in a second."

"Who can do that?"
       "This clear discernment."

"Where can you live safely then?"
       "In surrender."

"What is this giving up?"
       "A peace that saves us."

"Is there no threat of disaster?"
       "Only what comes in your street, inside your love."

"How do you walk there?"
       "In perfection."

Now silence. If I told more of this conversation,
those listening would leave themselves.

There would be no door,
no roof or window either!

Burnt Kabob

Last year, I admired wines. This,
I'm wandering inside the red world.

Last year, I gazed at the fire.
This year I'm burnt kabob.

Thirst drove me down to the water
where I drank the moon's reflection.

Now I am a lion staring up totally
lost in love with the thing itself.

Don't ask questions about longing.
Look in my face.

Soul-drunk, body-ruined, these two
sit helpless in a wrecked wagon.
Neither knows how to fix it.

And my heart, I'd say it was more
like a donkey sunk in a mudhole,
struggling and miring deeper.

But listen to me: for one moment,
quit being sad. Hear blessings
dropping their blossoms
around you. God.

Stories of Mevlana

Rumi was talking about the nature of humility. "Look at the trees. Those that yield no fruit—the pine, the cypress, the box—grow tall and conspicuous. Whereas those that give fruit—the apple, the peach, the pear—droop and trail their branches. Muhammed carried all the virtues, and yet he was more of a humble dervish than any other prophet. He had his head broken and his teeth knocked out. Still he prayed for those people "who know not what they do." Rumi always showed deep consideration for the least honored members of the community, the children and the old women. He always stopped to bless and be blessed by them, no matter if they were muslims or not. One day an Armenian butcher stopped on the road and bowed seven times to Jelaluddin, who immediately bowed seven times in return. Another day, he came upon some children playing a game. Some of them left their playing and came and bowed. Rumi acknowledged each as he would have an adult. And there was one little boy running across a field. "Wait! I'm coming!" Rumi stayed until the small one had come close and bowed and been bowed to.

It is said that Shams loved, and performed, the ecstatic meditation of dance. After Shams' disappearance Rumi used music and movement and spontaneous poetry to reintegrate Shams into his being. This is how Rumi's son, Sultan Velad, describes Mevlana's state:

> Day and night he danced in ecstasy. On earth he turned like the heavens. His cries reached into the sky, and everyone heard them. He showered gold and silver on the musicians. He gave away whatever he had. Never for a moment was he without music, and never at rest. In the city a protest grew.

Some were surprised that a great Qutb, the accepted leader of the two universes, should be raving like a madman in public and in private. But the great majority of the people in Konya turned away from conventional religious attitudes and went crazy after this ecstatic love. Poets of all sorts mingled freely with the musicians.

Shams returned to Rumi in the mixture of music and dance and poetry. Rumi was working in the art of transfiguration. Many of his poems took form while he was in the dance, often holding to a pillar and reciting as he moved around it, the circling being galactic and molecular and spiritual, a remembering of the cosmos and of the presence at the center.

Several citizens of Konya wrote theological and legal opinions against Rumi's use of music and dancing and song in his college. Out of kindliness and his generous understanding, Rumi made no reply, and after a while the objections diminished. Now there is no record of what they were.

One day someone asked, "What should be done with a young person who commits indecent acts?" Mevlana answered, "No matter. He is like a bird whose wings are growing. Those actions are signs that he will soon be fully fledged. More pitiful is one who leaves the nest before its wings are formed. One flap, and the cat has it."

Near the market, Rumi began talking to people in the late afternoon one day. A large crowd gathered, but as the sun went down and Jelaluddin kept discoursing, they wandered away. He went on into the night, until finally he was alone with a number of the town's stray dogs, who sat in a circle around him whining and wagging their tails. "You understand what I say," he announced to his canine audience. "Men have condescended and called you 'dogs,' but from now on, let your species be known as *the seven sleepers*, because of that blessed group in the *Qur'an*, which included one of you."

Some public figure commented, "Rumi is a great king of the spirit and a saint, but someone must separate him from those disciples!" When this was reported to Jelaluddin, he smiled, "If he can! My students are so disparaged among men, because they are such lovers of God. I have sifted humanity. Everyone has fallen through except these friends. My existence is the lives of these friends, and their existence is the lives of everyone else on this planet. Whether anyone is conscious of this or not, it is true."

Every year Rumi went for six weeks to a place near Konya where there were hot springs. Near a large lake there a music festival was arranged, and Rumi was to deliver a discourse. That day the ducks that lived on the lake were so vociferous that no could hear the talk. Finally Rumi yelled at them, "Either you give this discourse, or let me!" Complete silence ensued, and during the remaining weeks that Rumi was at the baths, no duck made a noise. When it came time for his return to Konya, Jelaluddin went to the edge of the water and gave them permission to quack as much as they wanted, whereupon the chattering resumed.

Some butchers had purchased a heifer. They were leading her to be slaughtered when she suddenly broke free and ran. They shouted at her, which made her more crazed, so that no one could get near. Rumi was walking the same road, with his disciples some distance behind. When the heifer saw him, she trotted over and stood beside him very still, as though communing with his spirit. Mevlana rubbed and patted her neck. When the butchers came to claim their property, he pleaded for her life. His students also joined in the discussion, and Rumi used the situation. "If a simple animal, being led to its death, can take such lovely refuge with me, how much more beautiful must it be when a human being puts heart and soul in the care of God?" The entire group, dervishes and butchers as well, found such joy in those words that music began to be played. Dancing and spontaneous poetry continued into the night, and there was a generous outpouring of alms and clothing for the poor.

Rumi's favorite flute player, Hamza, happened to die. Rumi sent some dervishes with grave-clothes to prepare the body. He himself came later to the house. As he entered the room, he spoke to Hamza, "Dear friend, get up!" And immediately Hamza sat up saying, "I'm here!" He reached for his flute, and for three days and nights sweet music came from that house. When Rumi left, life went from the corpse again, and he was buried.

Rumi said, "A secret is hidden in the rhythms of music. If I revealed it, it would upset the world." One afternoon a musician was playing the violin and Rumi was listening with great pleasure.

A friend entered and said, "Stop this. They are announcing the afternoon prayer." "No," said Rumi, "This is also the afternoon prayer. Both talk to God. He wants the one externally for his service and the other for his love and knowledge."

There was a hunchbacked tambourine player among Rumi's musicians. One night he was unusually ecstatic in his playing, bent over though he was. Jelaluddin himself felt transported. He went to the man and stroked his back. The tambourine player sat up straight, healed. When he returned home in this new posture, though, his wife refused to let him in the door, until companions testified to what had happened. The couple lived together for many years afterward.

The son of a professor returned to Konya from Mecca with many gifts for Jelaluddin and this amazing story. "We stopped to rest in the Arabian desert, and I fell asleep. When I woke, the caravan had gone. I was alone, and the wind had covered all traces of their tracks. I chose a direction at random and walked until I was completely exhausted. At that moment, to my great joy, I saw a tent in the distance with smoke rising from it. There was a man inside, calm and very dignified. He welcomed me and gestured that I should sit and rest. I told him my misadventures, and he smiled. There was a large kettle there with fresh stew simmering, and a vessel of cool spring water. 'What are these preparations for?' He replied, 'I am a disciple of Jelaluddin of Konya. He passes here every day. I pitch this tent and prepare food on the chance that he might bless me with his presence and have something to eat.' As he finished speaking, Rumi entered the tent. We bowed to each other, and he was invited to take some food. Rumi took a morsel no bigger than a filbert and gave one to me. I fell at his feet saying that I was on my way to Mecca from Konya, and I had fallen asleep and been separated from my caravan. 'Well, as we are fellow townsmen, there is nothing to worry about!' He asked me to close my eyes. I did, and when I opened them, I was walking in the midst of my companions on the way to Mecca. Now I have returned with these gifts to celebrate Mevlana's miraculous kindness."

After Shams' death Rumi was walking through the goldsmithing bazaar in Konya when the musical sounds of the hammering started him whirling in ecstasy. It is said that he turned for thirty-six hours before he sank to the street. "It wasn't me that fell," he said.

As he was dying, Mevlana told his disciples, "I have two attachments in this world, one to my body and the other to you. When, by grace, I am taken to the disembodied wholeness, this attachment to you will still exist."

Someone once said to Rumi, "If you believe in silence, why have you done nothing but talk and talk and write and sing and dance?" He laughed and said, "The radiant one inside me has never said a word."

Aflaki describes Rumi's funeral in Konya: After they had brought the corpse on a wooden pallet, everyone uncovered their heads. Women, men, children, rich and poor. Men were walking and crying and tearing open their robes. Members of all communities were present, Christian, Jews, Greeks, Arabs, Turks, and representatives from each were walking in front holding their holy books and reading aloud, from the *Psalms*, the *Gospels*, the *Qur'an*, the *Pentateuch*. The wild tumult was heard by the sultan, who sent to ask why the members of other religions were so moved. They answered, "We saw in Rumi the real nature of Christ and Moses and all the prophets. Just as you claim that he was the Muhammed of our time, we found in him the Jesus and the Moses. Did he not say, 'We are like a flute, which with a single mode is tuned to two hundred religions.' Mevlana is the sun of truth which has shone oneveryone." A Greek priest said, "Rumi is the bread which everyone needs to eat."

You push me into the dance.
You pull me by the ears like the ends
of a bow being drawn back.

You crush me in your mouth
like a piece of bread.
You've made me into *this*.

        I lay my forehead in the dust
        of your door, very near the end.

        Give me your mouth,
        so I can die out
        on your lips.

The early morning breeze tastes sweet
like the Friend. Rise and take that in,

before it dissipates in wasted energy, the many
preparations that caravans make to leave.

        The rider has passed, but his
        dust hangs in the air.

        Don't stare at these particles!
        The rider's direction is *there*.

Listen for the stream
that tells you one thing.

Die on this bank. Begin in me
the way of rivers with the sea.

There's no greater turbulence
than unhappy love. It's one
we may never recover from.

It's not cured by hypocrisy,
or courage. A true love

has nothing in it of power,
and nothing of faithfulness.

The world is an open green
in the middle of a garden.

Beings in various forms
see their reflections and laugh,
love-messages flashing from every eye.

If you have times you don't ache with love,
you shouldn't be here with us.

Try to stay pointed as a thorn,
so always at your side,
there'll be roses.

The one who is your being
and your non-being, the essence
inside joy and sadness—your eyes
must not see that one, else
you'd be completely that.

We don't have to follow
the pressure-flow of wanting.
We can be led by the guide.

Wishes may or may not come true
in this house of disappointment.

Let's push the door open
together and leave.

There's a path from me to you
I'm constantly looking for,

so I try to keep clear and still
as water does with the moon.

Longing is the core of mystery.
Longing itself brings the cure.
The only rule is, *Suffer the pain.*

Your desire must be disciplined,
and what you want to happen
in time, sacrificed.

While still yourself, you're shut off
from the two worlds. Ego-drunken-
ness cannot recognize either.

Only when you wash clean of both,
will the deep root of anger be cut.

If your guide is your ego,
don't rely on luck for help!

You sleep during the day,
and the nights are short.

By the time you wake up,
your life may be over!

Stay here today and tomorrow,
my Friend. Wait with me.

Generous and selfish actions,
both come as daylight.

Lovers take direct and also
wandering ways with no
treachery in either.

Each moment you call me to you
and ask how I am, even though you know.

The love I answer you with
stirs like wind through cypress.

Your love filled my chest, then emptied,
then came back to put its baggage down.

Now it's gone again. "Please,"
I called out. "Stay still
for a day or two."

So you sat down here with me,
and evidently have forgotten how to move.

I am a mountain.
You call, I echo.

This image that looks like me
was painted by the Friend.

You think I'm speaking these words?
When a key turns in a lock, the lock
makes a little opening sound.

Your presence is a river
that refreshes everyone,
a rosegarden fragrance.

Don't worry about making doorways
between individual lovers when
this flow is so all around.

They say I tell the truth.
Then they ask me to do a puppet show
of myself in the bazaar.

I'm not something to sell.
I have already been bought!

Some souls flow like clear water.
They pour into our veins
and feel like wine.

I give in to that. I fall flat.
We can sail this boat lying down!

Humble living does not diminish. It fills.
Going back to a simpler self gives wisdom.

When a man makes up a story for his child,
he becomes a father and a child
together, listening.

You don't win here with loud publicity.
Union comes of not being.
These birds do not learn to fly,
until they lose all their feathers.

Love enters, and the brilliant scholars
get goofy. The full moon becomes
a simple dirt road.
                    Walk there
with degenerates and saints, with
children and old people.

Be a slow pawn as well as
the wide-ranging queen,
then you'll be king.

Dear Soul

Dear soul, when the condition comes
that we call being a lover,
there's no patience, and no repenting.

Both become huge absurdities. See regret
as a worm and love as a dragon.

Shame, changeable weather. Love,
a quality which wants nothing.

For this kind of lover love
of anything or anyone is unreal.

Here, the source
and object are one.

A Small Green Island

There is a small green island
where one white cow lives alone,
a meadow of an island.

The cow grazes till nightfall, full and fat,
but during the night she panics
and grows thin as a single hair. "What shall I eat
tomorrow? There's nothing left!"

By dawn, the grass has grown up again, waist-high.
The cow starts eating and by dark
the meadow is clipped short.

She's full of strength and energy, but she panics
in the dark as before, and grows
abnormally thin overnight.

The cow does this over and over,
and this is all she does.

She never thinks, "This meadow has never failed
to grow back. Why should I be afraid
every night that it won't?"

The cow is the bodily soul.
The island field is this world where
that grows lean with fear and fat with blessing,

lean and fat. White cow,
don't make yourself miserable
with what's to come, or not to come.

Sheba's Throne

When the Queen of Sheba came to Solomon,
she left behind her kingdom and her wealth
the same way lovers leave their reputations.

Her servants meant nothing to her,
less than a rotten onion.

Her palaces and orchards,
so many piles of dung.

She heard the inner meaning of *LA!* No!
She came to Solomon with nothing, except
her throne! As the writer's pen becomes

a friend, as the tool the workman uses
day after day becomes deeply familiar, so
her filigreed throne was her one attachment.

I would explain more about this phenomenon,
but it would take too long.

It was a large throne and difficult to transport,
because it couldn't be taken apart, being as
cunningly put together as the human body.

Solomon saw that her heart was open to him
and that this throne would soon be repulsive
to her. "Let her bring it," he said. "It will

become a lesson to her like the old shoes
and jacket are to Ayaz. She can look at
that throne and see how far she's come."

In the same way, God keeps the process
of generation constantly before us:

the smooth skin and the semen
and the growing embryo.

When you see a pearl on the bottom,
you reach through the foam and broken sticks
on the surface. When the sun comes up, you forget
about locating the constellation of Scorpio.

When you see the splendor of union,
the attractions of duality seem poignant
and lovely, but much less interesting.

Say I Am You

I am dust particles in sunlight.
I am the round sun.

To the bits of dust I say, *Stay.*
To the sun, *Keep moving.*

I am morning mist,
and the breathing of evening.

I am wind in the top of a grove,
and surf on the cliff.

Mast, rudder, helmsman, and keel,
I am also the coral reef they founder on.

I am a tree with a trained parrot in its branches.
Silence, thought, and voice.

The musical air coming through a flute,
a spark off a stone, a flickering in metal.

Both candle and the moth crazy around it.
Rose and nightingale lost in the fragrance.

I am all orders of being,
the circling galaxy,

the evolutionary intelligence,
the lift and the falling away.

What is and what isn't. You
who know Jelaluddin, You

the One in all, say who
I am. Say I am You.

SOME SHORT POEMS FOUND IN SHAM'S *Maqalat* (DISCOURSES)
COMPOSED, PROBABLY, BY BOTH RUMI AND SHAMS

I, you, he, she, we.
In the garden of mystic lovers,
these are not true distinctions.

> From cane reeds, sugar.
> From a worm's cocoon, silk.
>
> Be patient if you can, and from sour
> grapes will come something sweet.

Morning breeze, bring news
of beauty. Slowly, please.
Let the fresh fragrance stay.

> Someone who doesn't make flowers makes thorns.
> If you're not building rooms where wisdom
> can be openly spoken, you're building a prison.

I went inside my heart
to see how it was.

Something there makes me hear
the whole world weeping.

Then I went to every city and small town,
searching for someone who could *speak* wisdom,
but everyone was complaining about love.

That moaning gave me an idea: *Go back inside
and find the answer.* But I found nothing.

The heart acts as translator between
mystical experience and intelligence.

It has its own inhabitants who do not talk
with someone just wandering through.

And remember that Muhammed said of the place
in human beings we call the heart,
This is what I value.

If I hold you with my emotions,
you'll become a wished-for companion.

If I hold you with my eyes,
you'll grow old and die.

So I hold you where we
both mix with the infinite.

How a Sheikh Is with a Community

Here is how a sheikh is with a community:
when you're inside the presence of a true human being,
it's like being on Noah's ark.

Muhammed said, "I am an ark in the flood
of time. You are the ones I'm carrying."

Even if asleep, you're still on board!
Don't try to survive without a teacher.

Sometimes your shiekh will be angry, sometimes kind.
Any attention is the same attention.

Sometimes he makes you green and quiet like the ground
in Spring, sometimes puffed up and arrogantly loud.

Sometimes he gives you dull, clay-like qualities,
so that roses and eglantine can grow,
flowers only the Friend sees.

Empty out your disbelief.
The transformation that's coming
will not be like a human being visiting
the moon, but more like the way sugarcane
becomes sugar. Not so much like
water vaporizing, more like

an embryo having its first rational thought.
Ride the horse of *fana*, and let it
change to Boraq!

Keep your soul moving toward its Friend.
No hands or feet are required for the going.

Just embark on this boat
and stay on it!

Many blessings from the unseen shower down
on the sheikh, as they do here on Husam!

When you give, gifts are given you,
a thousandfold. Inorganic matter
turns to visionary eloquence.

When you're generous with your love,
you're really loving yourself,
because what comes back in so amazing.

Creator of Absence and Presence

Mevlana was asked about a passage from the *Mathnawi*.

> Brother, you *are* that thought.
> Your bones and nerves are something else.
> (II,277)

He said, "Consider this. The word thought must be expanded
to mean *essence*, or it doesn't apply to what I'm saying there.
Everything that gets exchanged between people, whether it's
spoken or not, is a form of thought. Human beings are discourse.
The rest is blood and bones and nerves. Call it speech, that
flowing. Compare it to the sun, which is always warming us, even
when we can't see it. This speech-sun is invisible, except when
it takes form in language. God is extremely subtle, until these
gross bodies make *that* apparent. There was a certain man who
said that the word 'God' meant nothing to him. Then someone
began pointing to the *actions* of God, and he saw. There are people
who can't eat honey unless it's mixed with rice and turmeric.
The speech I'm describing is continuous like the sun's light and
heat. Usually we require a medium to enjoy it, but there are
ways to understanding *without* forms, an ocean of subtlety full of
miraculous beings and new colors.

This speech moves through you whether you say anything or not.
Philosophers claim, 'Man is the speaking animal.' And just as your
animality is always with you, so the speaking is constantly there.
Human beings live in three spiritual states. In the first, we pay
no attention to God. We notice only the stones and the dirt of
the world, the wealth, the children, the men and the women. In
the second, we do nothing but worship God. In the third, most
advanced state, we become silent. We don't say, 'I serve God,' or
'I don't serve.' We know that God is beyond being present or
absent. The creator of absence and presence! And other than both.

These opposites that generate each other are not qualities of God. There are no likenesses. God did not create God. When you reach this point, stop! At the edge of the ocean, footprints disappear. Language, science, all human skill, derives its relish from this speech. This flowing exchange gives flavor to every event. Like the man courting the wealthy woman, who owns large flocks of sheep and many horses and great orchards. He tends them. He waters the fruit trees and looks after the horses, but all the while he's thinking of the woman. If she were suddenly *not there*, his work would be distasteful and boring. Like that, everything that happens is filled with pleasure and warmth because of the delight of the discourse that's always going on, and if it weren't, nothing would have any meaning."

What Jesus Runs Away From

The son of Mary, Jesus, hurries up a slope
            as though a wild animal were chasing him.
Someone following him asks, "Where are you going?
            No one is after you." Jesus keeps on,
saying nothing, across two more fields. "Are you
            the one who says words over a dead person,
so that he wakes up?" I am. "Did you not make
            the clay birds fly?" Yes. "Who then
could possibly cause you to run like this?"
            Jesus slows his pace.

I say the Great Name over the deaf and the blind,
            and they are healed. Over a stony
mountainside, and it tears its mantle down to the navel.
            Over non-existence, it comes to existence.
But when I speak lovingly for hours, for days,
            with those who take human warmth
and mock it, when I say the Name to them, nothing
            happens. They remain rock, or turn to sand,
where no plants can grow. Other diseases are ways
            for mercy to enter, but this non-responding
breeds violence and coldness toward God.
            I am fleeing from that.

As little by little air steals water, so praise dries up
            and evaporates with foolish people who refuse
to change. Like a cold stone under your rump, a cynic
            steals body heat. He doesn't feel the sun.
Jesus wasn't running from actual people.
            He was teaching in a new way.

Omar and the Old Poet

The harper had grown old. His voice was choked-sounding
and harsh, and some of his harpstrings were broken.

He went to the graveyard at Medina and wept. "Lord,
you've always accepted counterfeit coins from me!
Take these prayers again, and give me enough
to buy new silk strings for my harp."

He put the harp down for a pillow and went to sleep.
The bird of his soul escaped! Free of the body
and the grieving, flying in a vast simple region
that was itself, where it could sing its truth.

"I love this having no head, this tasting without mouth,
this memory without regret, how without hands I gather
rose and basil on an infinitely stretching-out plain
that is my joy." So this waterbird plunged in its ocean,

Job's fountain where Job was healed of all afflictions,
the pure sunrise. If this *Mathnawi* were suddenly sky,
it could not hold half the mystery that this old poet
was enjoying in sleep. If there were a clear way
into that, no one would stay here!

The Caliph Omar, meanwhile, was napping nearby,
and a voice came, "Give seven hundred gold dinars
to the man sleeping in the cemetery."

Everyone understands this voice when it comes.
It speaks with the same authority to Turk and Kurd,
Persian, Arab, and Ethiopian, one language!

Omar went to the place and sat by the sleeping man.
Omar sneezed, and the poet sprang up thinking
this great man was there to accuse him.

"No. Sit here beside me. I have a secret to tell you.
There is gold enough in this sack to buy new silk
strings for your instrument. Take it,
buy them, and come back here."

The old man heard and realized the generosity
that had come. He threw the harp on the ground
and broke it. "These songs, breath by breath,

have kept me minding the musical modes of Iraq
and the rhythms of Persia. The minor *zirafgand*,
the liquid freshness of the twenty-four melodies,

these have distracted me while caravan after caravan
was leaving! My poems have kept me in my self,
which was the greatest gift to me, that now
I surrender back."

    When someone is counting out
gold for you, don't look at your hands,
or the gold. Look at the giver.

"But even this wailing recrimination," said Omar,
"is just another shape for enclosure, another joint
on the reed. Pierce the segments and be hollow,
with perforated walls, so flute music can happen.

Don't be a searcher wrapped in the importance of his quest.
Repent of your repenting!" The old man's heart
woke, no longer in love with treble
and bass, without weeping

or laughter. In the true bewilderment of the soul
he went out beyond any seeking, beyond words
and telling, drowned in the beauty,
drowned beyond deliverance.

Waves cover the old man.
Nothing more can be said of him.

He has shaken out his robe,
and there's nothing in it anymore.

There is a chase where a falcon dives into the forest
and doesn't come back up. Every moment,
the sunlight is totally empty
and totally full.

Husam

There is a way of passing away
from the personal, a dying
that makes one plural,
no longer single.

A gnat lights in buttermilk
to become nourishment for many.

Your soul is like that, Husam.
Hundreds of thousands of impressions
from the invisible world are eagerly wanting
to come through you! I get dizzy with the abundance.

When life is this dear, it means the source
is pulling us. Freshness comes from there.

We're given the gift of continuously dying
and being resurrected, ocean within ocean.

The body's death now to me is like going to sleep.
No fear of drowning, I'm in another water.
Stones don't dissolve in rain.

This is the end of the fifth book of the *Mathnawi*.
With constellations in the nightsky,
some look up and point.

Others can be guided by the arrangements:
the Sagittarian bow piercing enemies.
The waterjar soaking the fruit trees.
The bull plowing and sowing its truth.
The lion tearing the darkness robe open
to red satin. Use these words to change.

Be kind and honest, and harmful
poisons will turn sweet inside you.

Road Dust

This poem has no way of ending!

You ask for Zayd. To warn him
not to become famous?

Don't try to constellate
the milk in the Milky Way!

It's all one obliterated smear,
mystics lost in the ocean.

Night comes, and the familiar outlines
assume their duties, a dancing crowd
with rings of knowledge in their ears,
crumbled ancestors, the road dust
of horsemen rising into shapes.

The Pick-Axe

Some commentary on *I was a hidden treasure,
and I desired to be known:* tear down

this house. A hundred thousand new houses
can be built from the transparent yellow carnelian

buried beneath it, and the only way to get to that
is to do the work of demolishing and then

digging under the foundations. With that value
in hand all the new construction will be done

without effort. And anyway, sooner or later this house
will fall on its own. The jewel treasure will be

uncovered, but it won't be yours then. The buried
wealth is your pay for doing the demolition,

the pick and shovel work. If you wait and just
let it happen, you'll bite your hand and say,

"I didn't do as I knew I should have." This
is a rented house. You don't own the deed.

You have a lease, and you've set up a little shop,
where you barely make a living sewing patches

on torn clothing. Yet only a few feet underneath
are two veins, pure red and bright gold carnelian.

Quick! Take the pick-axe and pry the foundation.
You've got to quit this seamstress work.

What does the patch-sewing *mean* you ask. Eating
and drinking. The heavy cloak of the body

is always getting torn. You patch it with food,
and other restless ego-satisfactions. Rip up

one board from the shop floor and look into
the basement. You'll see two glints in the dirt.

Root, River, Fire, Sea

A man was wandering the marketplace at noon
with a candle in his hand, totally ecstatic.

"Hey," called a shopkeeper. "Is this a joke?
Who are you looking for?" "Someone breathing *Huuuuuu*,

the divine breath." "Well, there are plenty
to choose from." "But I want one who can be

in anger and desire and still a true human being
in the same moment." "A rare thing! But maybe

you're searching among the branches for what appears
only in the roots." There's a river that turns

these millstones. Human will is an illusion. Those
that are proud of deciding things and carrying out
decisions are the rawest of the raw! Watch the thought-
kettles boiling and then look down at the fire.

God said to Job, "You value your patience well.
Consider now that I gave you that patience."

Don't be absorbed with the waterwheel's motion.
Turn your head and gaze at the river. You say,

"But I'm looking there already." There are several signs
in eyes that see all the way to the ocean. Bewilderment

is one. Those who study foam and flotsam near the edge
have purposes, and they'll explain them at length!

Those who look out to sea become the sea,
and they can't speak about that. On the beach

there's desire-singing and rage-ranting,
the elaborate language-dance of personality,

but in the waves and underneath there's no volition,
no hypocrisy, just love forming and unfolding.

What Are Words Anyway?

There is a parrot in you that God speaks through.
What the parrot says, you see reflected

in phenomena. The parrot takes away what you think
you like and gives joy. She hurts you and you feel

the perfect justice of the pain. You were burning
up your soul to keep the body delighted,

but you didn't know what you were doing. I am
another kind of fire. If you have trash

to get rid of, bring it here. My kindling is always
on the verge of catching. How can such things be

hidden? How can I talk with a raging lion inside me?
The lion that wants union cannot be contained by

any meadow. I try to think of different rhyme-words,
but the Friend says, "Think only of me. Sit and rest

in my presence, where you yourself rhyme with me!
What are words anyway? Thorns in the hedge

that goes around the vineyard. I'll make word-sounds
unintelligible. I can talk to you without them!

You are the consciousness of the world, and I want
to tell you what I didn't tell Adam, or Abraham,

what Jesus held back from saying." Language has been
qualified up until now with signifiers denoting

positive and negative. No more of that. The true self
is a no-self. Fall in love with the lover who

disappears in a love for you. Be water searching
for thirst. Be silent and all ear. When Spring

ecstasy floods, build a dam or everything will wash
away. Oh let it go! Under the foundation's ruins

there's treasure. Those drowned in God want to be
more drowned. They can't decide, being thrown

about, whether they love more the bottom,
the surface, or some middle region.

A Salve Made with Dirt

I was a thorn rushing to be
with a rose, vinegar blending
with honey, a pot of poison turning
to healing salve, the pasty
wine-dregs thrown into whitewater.

I was a diseased eye reaching
for Jesus' robe, raw meat
cooking in the flame.

Then I found some dust
to make an ointment of
that would honor my soul,

and in mixing that,
I found poetry.

Love says, "You are right,
but don't claim those changes.

Remember, I am the wind.
You are an ember
I ignite."

A Story They Know

It's time for us to join the line
of your madmen, all chained together.

Time to be totally free,
and estranged.

Time to give up our souls.
To set fire to structures
and run out in the street.

Time to ferment. How else
can we leave the world-vat
and go to the lip?

We must die to become
true human beings.

We must turn completely upsidedown
like a comb in the top
of a beautiful woman's hair.

Spread out your wings as a tree lifts
in the orchard. A seed scattered
on the road, a stone melting to
wax, a candle becoming moth.

On the chessboard, a king
is blessed again with its queen.

With our faces so close to the love-mirror,
we must not breathe, but change
to a cleared place where a building was
and feel the treasure hiding inside us.

With no beginning or end we live
in lovers as a story they know.

If you will be the key,
we'll be tumblers in the lock.

Talking in the Night

In the middle of the night,
I cried out,
        "Who lives in this love
I have?"
        You said, "I do, but I'm not here
alone. Why are these other images
with me?"
        I said, "They are reflections of you,
just as the beautiful inhabitants of Chigil
in Turkestan resemble each other."

You said, "But who is this other *living*
being?"
        "That is my wounded soul."

Then I brought that soul
to you as a prisoner.
                "This one is dangerous,"
I said. "Don't let him off easy."

You winked and gave me one end
of a delicate thread.
                "Pull it tight,
but don't break it."
                I reached my hand
to touch you. You struck it down.

"Why are you so harsh with me?"

"For good reason. But certainly not
to keep you away! Whoever enters this place
saying *Here I am* must be slapped.

This is not a pen for sheep.
There are no separating distances here.
This is love's sanctuary.

Saladin is how the soul looks. Rub your eyes,
and look again with love at love."

Leave Childhood

Why doesn't the soul fly
when it hears the call?

A fish on the beach always
moves toward wave-sound.

A falcon hears the drum
and brings its quarry home.

Why doesn't every dervish
dance in the sun?

You've escaped the cage.
Your wings are stretched
out. Now, fly!

You've stayed in sheds and out-buildings
so long you think that's where you live!

How many years, like children,
do we have to collect sticks and pieces
of broken pottery and pretend they're valuable?

Let's leave childhood and go
to the banquet of free human beings.

Split open the cultural mould.
Put your head up out of the sack.

Hold this book in the air
with your right hand. Are you old enough
to know your right from your left?

God said to clarity,
                    Walk,

and to death,
                Help them with discipline.
To the soul,
               Move into the invisible.
Take what's there,
                  and don't sing
the pain anymore.
             Call out that
you are now the king.

You have been given both the answer
and an understanding of the question.

Harvest

As the sun goes down in its well,
lovers enter the seclusion of God.

Late at night we meet like thieves
who have stolen gold, our
candlelit faces.

A pawn has become a king.
We sit secretly inside presence
like a Turk in a tent among the Hindus,

and yet we're traveling past
a hundred watchmen, nightfaring,
drowned in an ocean of longing.

Sometimes a body rises to the surface
like Joseph coming out of his well
of abandonment to be the clarity

that divides Egypt's wheat fairly
and interprets the royal dreaming.

Some people say about human beings,
Dust to dust, but can that be true of
one who changes from road dust to doorway?

The crop appears to be all one thing,
while it's still in the field.

Then a transformation-time arrives,
and we see how it is: half
chaff, half grain.

Joseph

Joseph has come,
the handsome one of this age,
a victory banner floating over Spring flowers.

Those of you whose work it is
to wake the dead, get up!
This is a work day.

The lion that hunts lions charges into the meadow.
Yesterday and the day before are gone.

The beautiful coin of now
slaps down in your hand.

The streets and buildings of this city
are all saying, *The prince is coming!*

Start the drumbeat. Everything we've said
about the Friend is true. The beauty of that
peacefulness makes the whole world restless.

Spread your love-robe out to catch
what sifts down from the ninth level.

You strange, exiled bird with clipped wings,
now you have four full-feathered pinions.

You heart closed up in a chest, open,
for the Friend is entering you.

You feet, it's time to dance!
Don't talk about the old man.

He's young again. And don't mention
the past. Do you understand?
The Beloved is *here!*

You mumble,
              "But what excuse can I give the king?"
when the king is here making excuses to you!

You say, "How can I escape his hand?"
when that hand is trying to help you.

You saw a fire, and light came.
You saw blood, and wine
is being poured.

Don't run from your own tremendous good fortune.

Be silent and don't try
to add up what's been given.

An uncountable grace has come to you.

Keep Moving

Do you hear what the violin
says about longing?

The same as the stick, "I was once
a green branch in the wind."

We are all far from home.
Language is our caravan bell.

Don't stop anywhere.
The moment you're attracted to a place,
you grow bored with it.

Think of the big moves you've already made,
from a single cell to a human being!

Stay light-footed, and keep moving.
Turkish, Arabic, Greek, any tongue
is a wind that was formerly water.

As a breeze carries the ocean inside it,
so underneath every sentence is,
Come back to the source.

A moth doesn't avoid flame.
The king lives in the city.

Why should I keep company with an owl
out here in the empty buildings?

If your donkey acts crazy and won't work,
apply the bullwhip to his head.
He'll understand.

Don't try to love him
back to his senses. Whack him!

Shams' Way of Talking

Rumi's son, Sultan Velad, describes how it was to be with Shams: "When he spoke of the *Qur'an* and the sayings of Muhammed, he sowed new love in my soul, and he revealed secrets. He made me fly without wings and reach the ocean with no boundaries, where I found peace and, like a bird freed from a trap, felt safe from all dangers." *(Velednama)*

When Shams returned to Konya on May 8, 1247, Rumi spoke this poem:

> Shams is wine, but not the kind
> that muddles and brings regret.
>
> Shams is music and light and fire.
> He brings the majesty that lives
> in the deep center of everyone.

The following are excerpts from Shams' *Maqalat*, his discourses:

One day a minor court official spilled food on the king's robe. The king ordered the man to be hanged, whereupon he dumped the entire platter on the king. Laughing and amazed, the king, "Why?" "You were going to hang me for a trivial mishap. I thought I'd give you more reason for your action. Then if you decide to show clemency, your mercy will also be greater."

A man was describing a large fish. "Wait a minute," said another. "How do you know anything about fish?" "I have taken many boatrides," said the first. "Say something *specific* about fish." "They have horns like a camel." The other responded, "Well, I knew you didn't know anything about fish. Now I see you can't tell a camel from a cow."

A great caravan arrived at a certain place where they found no habitation and no water. There was a deep well, but no bucket and no rope. To test for fresh water, they tied a kettle to a rope of their own and let it down. It struck something, and they pulled, but the kettle broke away. They sent down another and lost it too. After that they lowered thirsty volunteers from the caravan, but they also disappeared.

There was a wise man there. He said, "I will go down." He was nearly to the bottom when a terrible dark creature appeared. "I can never escape from you," said the man to the monster, "but I hope at least to stay aware, so I can see what's happening to me."

"Don't tell me long stories! You're my prisoner. You'll never leave unless you answer one question."

"Ask it."

"Where is the best place?"

The wise man reflected, "I am totally helpless here. If I say Baghdad or some other beautiful place, it may be that I will insult his hometown by not mentioning it." So he replied, "The best place for someone to live is where he feels at home. If that's a hole in the middle of the earth, then that's it."

"Well said. You are a rare human being. Because of your blessing, I'll set the others free in your care and give you authority over the world. I'll take no more prisoners, and I'll release the waters of this well."

I tell this story for the inner meaning, which might be phrased in other ways, but those attached to traditional forms will accept this version. They're hard to talk to. Tell just a slightly different parable, and they won't listen at all.

People say that human beings are microcosms and this outer universe a macrocosm, but for us the outer is a tiny wholeness and the inner life the vast reality.

Lovers of God do the ecstatic dance to be with God. There is another kind of physical dance that does not intend that, but do not think so of the *sema*.

I have nothing to do with mundane concerns. I have come to be with and put my finger on the nerves of those who guide others to God.

Should I lie, or speak openly? All right. Rumi is the moon. I am the sun. People can look directly at the moon, but not at the sun.

One tiny speck of dirt inside the spirit is a hundred times worse than any outside dirt.

People love hypocrisy. I said to a certain man, "You are unique, one of the great beings on the planet." He took my hand, "I have been meaning to come see you, and now finally." The year before, when I told him the truth about himself, he hated me. If you want to live easily with people, be a hypocrite. If you want to say truth, go to a desert mountain.

The Kaaba is in the middle of the world. All faces turn toward it. But if you take it away, you'll see that each is worshipping the soul of each.

God enters the love we have for each other, stays there, and will not leave to go to any so-called "house of God," kaaba, temple, church, or sacred grove.

Mevlana knows that the writer wrote in three scripts:
>One that he could read and only he,
>one that he and others could read, and one
>that neither he nor anyone else could
>read. I am that third script.

A King Dressed As a Servant

A sweet voice calls out,
"The caravan from Egypt is here!"
A hundred camels with what amazing treasure!

Midnight, a candle and someone quietly
waking me, "Your Friend has come."

I spring out of my body, put a ladder to the roof,
and climb up to see if it's true.

Suddenly, there is a world within this world!
An ocean inside the waterjar!
A king sitting with me wearing the uniform of a servant!
A garden in the chest of the gardener!

I see how love has "thoughts,"
and that these thoughts are circling
in conversation with majesty.
Let me keep opening this moment
like a dead body reviving.

Shamsi Tabriz saw the placeless one
and from That, made a place.

Listening

Another year, another Spring!
The fragrance of love arrives.

So dancy, this new light
on the ground, and in the tree.

The one who heals us
lets whatever hurts the soul

dissolve to a listening
intelligence, where what we most

deeply want, union with eternity,
grows up around and inside us now!

When a Sheikh Weeps

Someone asked a mystic, "If tears come
            as I am praying, does this
deepen the prayer?"
                        "It depends on
why you cry. If it's a longing
            for God, that fresh spring rising
inside you, then the mourning is real,
            but if it's for some loss you feel,
the thread snaps, the spindle flies off.
            Even the love you have for your child,
even grief for that loss, as Abraham
            was told to sacrifice Isaac,
breaks the connection. When a sheikh
            weeps, it's not like other weeping."

Inhale Autumn, Long for Spring

Union is a watery way. In an eye, the point
of light. In the chest, the soul.

I don't deserve to be with you.
Your grace draws me.

The place where ecstatic lovers go
is called the tavern, where everyone gambles,
and whoever loses has to live there.

So, my love, even if you're the pattern
of time's orderly passage, don't go!
Or if you do, wear a disguise!

But don't cover your chest.
Keep open there.

Someone asked me, "What is love?"
Don't look for an explanation.

Dissolve into me and you'll know when it calls.
Respond! Walk out as a lion, a rose.
Inhale autumn, long for Spring.

You that change the dull field,
who give conversation to damaged ears,
make dying alive, award guardianship
to the wandering mind, you,

who erase the five senses at night,
who give eyes allure and a bloodclot wisdom,
who give the lover heroic strength,

you who hear what Sanai said, "Lose
your life, if you're seeking eternity."

The master who teaches us
is absolute light, not
this visibility.

The Oil of the Nut

The king asked his faithful servant Ayaz
to give some judgment on the accusers
who had broken into his room and found only
Ayaz' old workboots and tattered sheepskin jacket.

Ayaz delayed his decision, but when the king urged
him for a quick resolution, Ayaz answered,

"All command is yours. What is Venus, Mercury,
or the rare appearance of a comet
when the sun is out?

I hesitate to blame anyone in this.
If I had not done this strange honoring
of my old dirt clothes, I would not have
triggered the imaginations of these
who love to look for faults.

Doing that with me, though, is reaching
into the river to find a dry clod.
How can a fish betray the sea?

They were looking for some mistrust in one
whose enveloping element is trust."

I would comment on Ayaz' words
if I didn't know how many are waiting
to misquote my comments and cause confusion.

There's a voice that doesn't use words.
Listen to it, as the personal self
breaks open. Taste a silence

in the oil of the nut, that sweet joy,
the reason we bother at all with
these rattling-walnut words.

Get to the ecstatic dumbness inside poetry
and discourses on mystery. One
day, try not speaking!

These Poems Are Elusive

For the grace of the presence, be grateful.
Touch the cloth of the robe, but don't pull it
toward you, or like an arrow it will leave the bow!

Images! Presence plays with form,
fleeing and hiding as sky does in water.

Now one place, now nowhere.
Imagination cannot contain the absolute.
These poems are elusive because that presence is.

I love the rose that is not a rose,
but the second I try to speak it, any name
for God becomes so & so. It vanishes.

What you thought to draw lifts off the paper,
as what you love slips from your heart.

A Green-Winged Longing

This world of two gardens, and both so beautiful.
This world, a street where a funeral is passing.
Let us rise together and leave "this world,"

as water goes bowing down itself to the ocean.
From gardens to the gardener, from grieving
to wedding feast. We tremble like leaves

about to let go. There's no avoiding pain,
or feeling exiled, or the taste of dust.

But also we have a green-winged longing
for the sweetness of the Friend.

These forms are evidence of what
cannot be shown. Here's how it is

to go into that: rain that's been leaking
into the house decides to use the downspout.

The bent bowstring straining at our throats
releases and becomes the arrow!

Mice quivering in fear of the housecat suddenly
change to half-grown lion cubs, afraid of nothing.

So let's begin the journey home,
with love and compassion for guides,
and grace protecting. Let your soul turn

into an empty mirror that passionately wants
to reflect Joseph. Hand him your present.

Now let silence speak, and as that
gift begins, we'll start out.

A Light Within His Light

I circled awhile with each of the intelligences,
the nine fathers that control the levels
of spirit-growth. I revolved

for years with the stars through
each astrological sign.

I disappeared into the kingdom of nearness.
I saw what I have seen, receiving nourishment
as a child lives in the womb.

Personalities are born once,
a mystic many times.

Wearing the body-robe, I've been busy
in the market, weighing and arguing prices.

Sometimes I have torn the robe off
with my own hands and thrown it away.

I've spent long nights in monasteries,
and I have slept with those who claim to believe
nothing on the porches of pagodas,
just traveling through.

When someone feels jealous, I am inside
the hurt and need to possess.

When anyone is sick, I feel
feverish and dizzy.

I am cloud and rain being released,
and then the meadow as it soaks it in.

I wash the grains of mortality
from the cloth around a dervish.

I am the rose of eternity, not made of
water or fire or the wandering wind,
or even earth. I play with those.

I am not Shams of Tabriz,
but a light within his light.

If you see me, be careful.
Tell no one what you've seen.

The Inward Dance

Sacrifice your mind
to be with the Friend.

You do have a spiritual guide,
in whose presence you move
with fresh intelligence.

It's not like "thinking."
There's no effort.

Your field sprouts subtle discourse.
Orchards give out lusciousness
with little ostentation.

Move quietly and as the Friend moves.
Some let a lower wanting lead them
as a scorpion does with his tail.

Crooked, night-blind, ugly, and poisonous,
they delight only in wounding one
who loves the inward dance.

Eyes

That sweet-tongued spirit-king, Hakim Sanai,
used to say that every hair on a mystic's body
becomes an eye. He didn't mean ordinary sight.
Some seeing does not depend on that mechanism.

You saw in the womb, and you see in dream
without opening eyelids, but there is a connection.

As birds ride air. As Adam means earth
and came out of it to glorify the ground.
As Egypt's illness grew Moses to heal it.
As a brittle gourd-cup holds sweet wine.

So eyes receive the invisible, and the mixing
of their filmy substance with that
is love's great mystery.

Divan, Mathnawi, AND *Discourses* REFERENCES::

Divan: A Trace, #100; The Waterwheel, #359; Any Chance Meeting, #19;
Spring, #211; You who long for powerful positions, #188; Soul of this world,
#183; Not until a person dissolves, #604; Your eyes are the mystery, #632;
The Source of Joy, #423; Looking for the ocean, #622; Some souls flow like
clear water, #504; Humble living does not diminish, #397; You don't win here
with loud publicity, #553; Talking Through the Door, #436; Keep Moving,
#304; They say I tell the truth, #496; Love enters, and the brilliant scholars,
#1581; While still yourself, #605; Longing itself brings the cure, #191; We
don't have to follow, #554; The one who is your being, #1597; There's a
path from me to you, #185; If your guide is your ego, #608; A Salve Made
with Dirt, #1586; A Story They Know, #1649; Joseph, #707; Harvest, #524;
Leave Childhood, #1353; Talking in the Night, #1335; A King Dressed As a
Servant,#2730; Inhale Autumn, Long for Spring, #2737; These Poems are
Elusive, #900; A Green-Winged Longing, #1713; A Light Within His Light,
#331.

Mathnawi and Discourses: Love Dogs, III, 189-211; Majnun with Layla's Dog,
III, 567-575; The One Thing You Must Do, Discourse #4; Flag-Lions, IV,
3051-3054, 3059-3084; Personal Intelligence, IV, 1294-1300; A Zero-Circle,
IV, 3748-3754; The Sign of Being Dried Up, VI, 2230-2233, 2239-2246; Be
Suspicious of Yourself, VI, 418-434; What Hurts the Soul? I, 3684-3692;
The Guest-House, V, 3644-3646, 3676-3680, 3693-3695; The Reed
Flute's Song, I, 1-18; The Animal Soul, IV, 1943-1959; The Womb, VI,
3416-3421; Needle and Thread, II, 3325-3335; The Water You Want, IV,
3226-3241; Father Reason, IV, 3259-3270; Hypothesis and Human Being, IV,
3836-3842,3847-3855; Polishing the Mirror, II, 2059, 2061, 2068-2094; A
Star Without a Name, III, 1284-1288; Dear Soul, VI, 969-971; A Small Green
Island, V, 2855-2865; Sheba's Throne, IV, 863-889; How a Sheikh Is with a
Community, IV, 538-562; Creator of Absence and Presence, Discourse #53;
What Jesus Runs Away From, III, 2570-2598; Omar and the Old Poet, I,
2076, 2086-2101, 2106-2109, 2163-2166, 2175-2220; Husam, V, 4204-4238;
Road Dust, I, 3667-3676; The Pick-Axe, IV, 2540-2559; Root, River, Fire,
Sea, V, 2887-2911; What Are Words Anyway? I, 1717-1746; Shams' story
about the monster in the well is from Rumi's Discourse #18; When a Sheikh
Weeps, V, 1265-1271; The Oil of the Nut, V, 2134-2149; The Inward Dance,
IV, 1424-1431; Eyes, IV, 2401-2406, 2408-2413, 2420-2424.